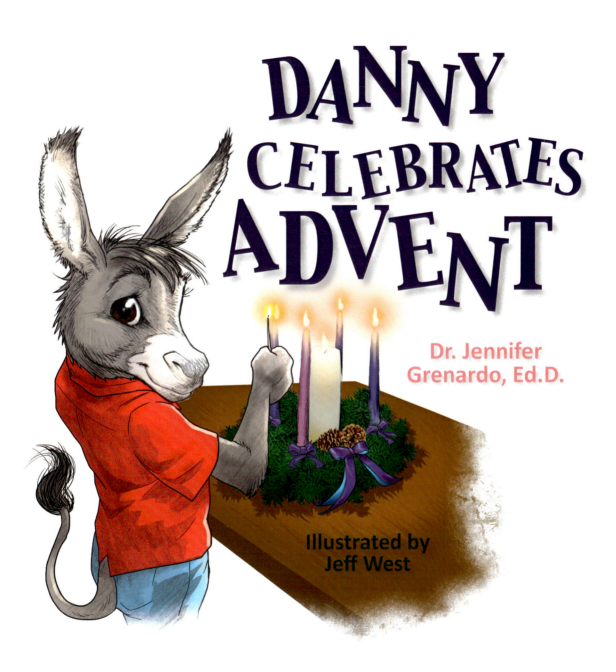

Danny Celebrates Advent
Dr. Jennifer Grenardo, Ed.D.

Illustrated by Jeff West

Copyright © 2013, Jennifer Grenardo, All rights reserved.

Cover and book design: Tau Publishing Design Department

Nihil Obstat granted on September 13, 2013 by the Very Rev. Lawrence J. Christian, Vicar General, Archdiocese of San Antonio, Texas.

No part of this book may be reproduced, stored in a retrieval system or transmitted in any form or by any means - electronic, mechanical, photocopying, recording, or otherwise - without written permission of the publisher.

For information regarding permission, write to:
Tau Publishing, LLC
Attention: Permissions Dept.
4727 North 12th Street
Phoenix, AZ 85014

ISBN 978-1-61956-179-3

Second Edition September 2013
10 9 8 7 6 5 4 3 2

Published and printed in the United States of America by Tau Publishing, LLC
For additional inspirational books visit us at TauPublishing.com

TauPublishing.com
Words of Inspiration

For My "Three Boys"
—David, Solomon, and Moses

My name is Danny.
I'm a donkey, you see.
I celebrate Advent
With my whole family.

A LONG TIME AGO,
Mary traveled so far.
My ancestor carried her
And saw a bright star.

TODAY WE CELEBRATE
Her journey and more,
Especially Baby Jesus,
The child she bore.

MY FAMILY PREPARES
Our hearts for the season
With traditions and crafts
For Jesus, the reason.

Mommy and Daddy,
Brother, Sister, and me,
We prepare for His coming,
Four weeks, patiently.

WE START WITH OUR ADVENT WREATH,
There's purple everywhere.
We light candles and make crafts,
For God's love we will share.

Our Advent Wreath Has Four Candles.
Daddy lights them so bright.
Purple, purple, pink, purple,
They shine through the night.

We then make a manger
For Baby Jesus, His bed.
When we do a good deed,
Mommy puts in hay for His head.

PRAYERS AND SYMBOLS
Of the Jesse Tree are fun.
Grandpa reads from the Bible
How God loves everyone.

GRANDMA HELPS MAKE AN ANGEL,
Who appeared to Mother Mary.
The angel brought her peace
As Baby Jesus she carried.

Advent season is over,
And purple is done.
We celebrate with white
For the birth of God's Son.

On Christmas Day, we go to Mass
To celebrate Baby Jesus.
The priest wears white and says,
"Oh, how His love has freed us!"

Advent and Christmas
Are our favorite times, we cheer!
We fill our hearts with love and joy
To share throughout the year.

ADVENT PAPER PLATE PROJECTS

Week 1:
Advent Wreath

1. Cut out the center of a paper plate to make a doughnut shape.
2. Color the doughnut shape green to make a wreath.
3. Around the wreath, tape 3 purple candles and 1 pink candle made out of construction paper.
4. Each week tape a flame (cut out of yellow construction paper) onto a different candle in this order: purple, purple, pink, purple.

When all of the candles are lit, it will be time to celebrate Jesus' birthday, just like a birthday cake!

* For older children, write the words or draw a symbol denoting the meaning for each candle.

1. Smiley face symbol or "HOPE"
2. Cross symbol or "FAITH"
3. Heart symbol or "LOVE"
4. Peace symbol or "PEACE"

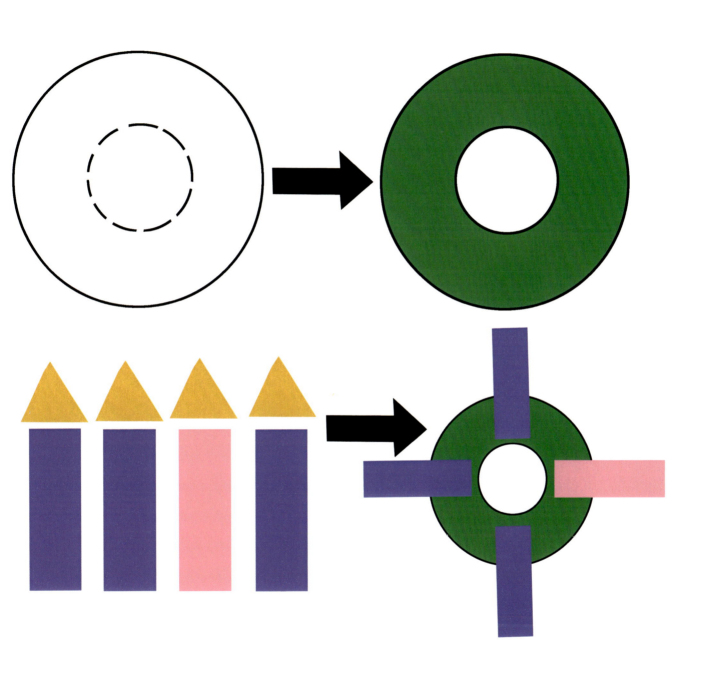

Week 2:

Jesus' Manger

1. Color a paper plate brown.
2. Cut four slits around the edges.
3. Fold the edges over each other and tape them together with a flattened bottom to make a manger.

Every time your child does something kind or thoughtful, place a piece of cotton or hay into the manger. This will help your child see how doing good works shows our love for Jesus by softening His bed.

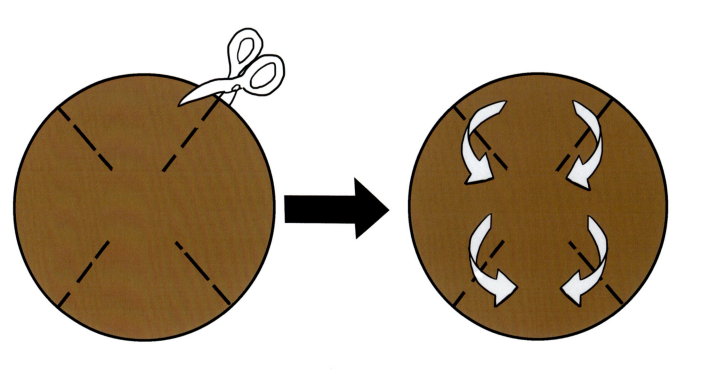

Week 3:

Jesse Tree

1. Color a paper plate green.
2. Cut one slit in the plate from the edge to the center.
3. Fold the plate into a cone shape and tape.
4. Cut a star out of construction paper and tape it to the top of the tree.

Tape different ornaments on the tree that correspond with a story from the Bible.

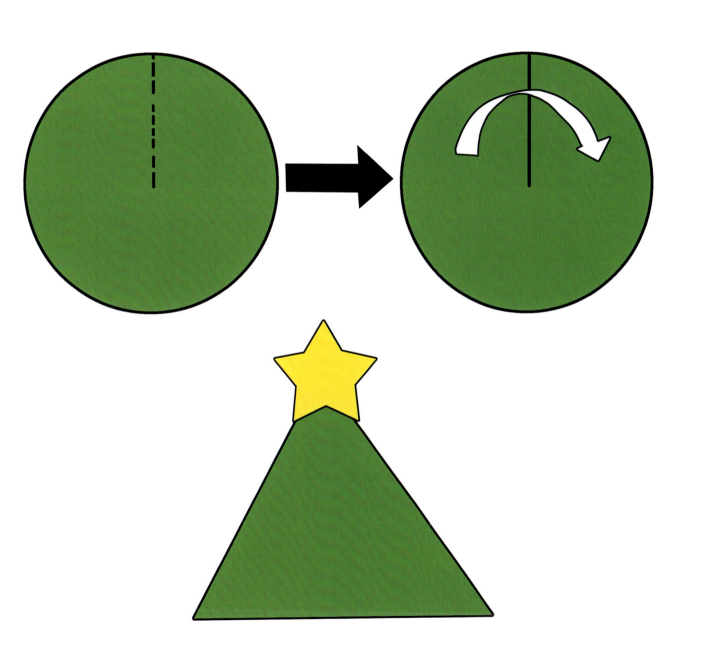

Week 4:

The Angel Gabriel

1. Cut a paper plate into two halves.
2. Fold one half of the plate into a cone shape and tape.
3. Tape the other half of the plate onto the back of the cone as wings.
4. Draw a face on a circular piece of paper and tape it to the top of the cone.
5. Feel free to add a golden halo out of pipe cleaners or glitter.

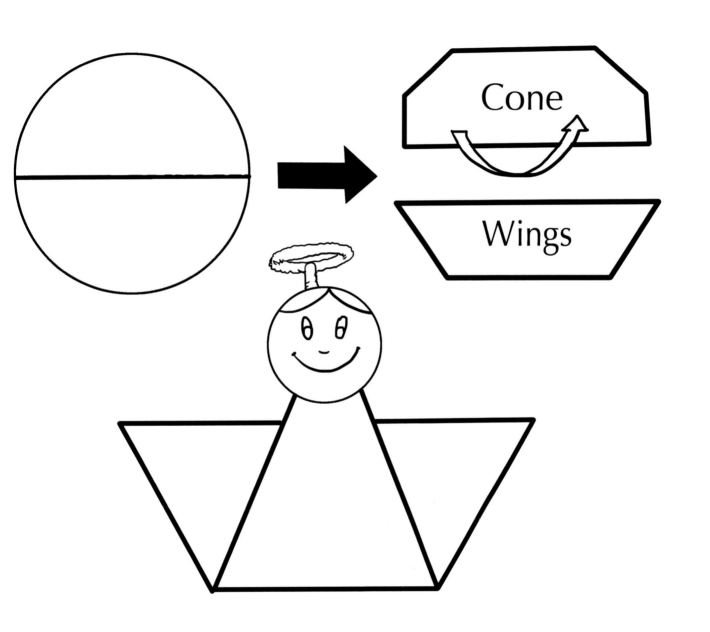

About the Author

Dr. Jennifer Grenardo earned her Doctorate of Education from Loyola Marymount University in Los Angeles. She was formerly a teacher and principal at Catholic elementary and middle schools. Dr. Grenardo also designed and directs a faith formation program for toddlers (ages zero to five) and their parents. Dr. Grenardo, her husband, and two sons currently reside in San Antonio, Texas.